"I UNDERSTAND . . .
YOU FORGOT TO SAY GOODBYE"

FAMILY MEMOIRS ON LIVING WITH A
PARENT WHO HAD ALZHEIMER'S

ROBERT L. PACE

ISBN 978-1-64258-396-0 (paperback)
ISBN 978-1-64258-397-7 (digital)

Christian Faith Publishing, Inc.
832 Park Avenue
Meadville, PA 16335
www.christianfaithpublishing.com

Printed in the United States of America

This book is a collection of memories, events, and observations from my family, during the care of our mother as she lived with Alzheimer's. Our expectation is that our sharing will assist others in the interactions with their parents or loved ones with Alzheimer's.

In loving memory of Luella Pace, who fought
so courageously during her journey.
Every member of the family, near and far, remembers how she was
able to touch lives in such a loving and caring manner that left
a lasting impact that will always bring a smile to our faces . . .
With all the love we have, we say thank you and
most of all we love you and miss you!

Contents

Family Acknowledgment

The most any person could wish for is a strong, loving, and supportive family. The family support was from far and near. To that end, each person knows what they contributed, and for that reason, a big hug and sincere appreciation is noted now. Each one of you provided loving support—thank you!

Message from Our Family

It is our sincerest hope that our sharing in this book will ignite a single item or multiple items that will assist those who may have a parent or loved one with Alzheimer's. We are not offering a blueprint for magical ingredients for the creation of a cure, but mostly providing points encountered that may be useful to you in your current care of your loved one. We recognize each case is different, yet there can be some similar items that our experiences may assist the next family.

We have included writing space on each page, as we believe this will assist you in documenting quick notes for future reference. Those notes will be accessible for visiting and revisiting during the course of care of your parent or loved one.

We also believe that our mother would be pleased to know we attempted to help others on this journey—so that is the reason we have put pen to paper and cover a variety of topics. No, no solutions, but merely sharing from our family to you!

By all means, understand and follow the guidance of the legal and financial professionals you have engaged. This process is the same for the medical team you have engaged for the delivery of medical services for your loved one.

Reader's Notes

• • •

Use this section to capture your initial thoughts before reading the book, to help identify your concerns and what you hope to get from the reading of this book. Remember this is a journey, and having notes along the way will be useful . . .

_____
_____
_____
_____
_____
_____
_____
_____
_____
_____
_____
_____
_____
_____
_____
_____
_____
_____
_____
_____
_____
_____
_____
_____
_____
_____
_____

Pictures of Our Mother— Book's Inspiration

Sunrise: December 27, 1925, Sunset: October 26, 2016

Pictures of Our Mother—
Book's Inspiration

Understanding Alzheimer's

The first item our family quickly had to grasp was the disease itself . . . What is Alzheimer's?

We had no idea what it was and initially could not spell it correctly. What was our course of action? "Let's Google it." Using Google as a verb was the start of our knowledge journey. Thinking back, we did not leverage joining any support groups as a casual observer nor did we even talk very loudly in the family about it. I believe now our pride stopped us, as we could feel and see a slight difference but did not want to bring forward the thought.

Using the Internet and searching for Alzheimer's, a host of items will be returned. The information below is just an example of the information that can be obtained when conducting your own research.

I. *Alzheimer's is the most common form of dementia*, a general term for memory loss and other intellectual abilities, serious enough to interfere with daily life.

II. *Alzheimer's has no current cure, but treatments for symptoms are available and research continues.* Although current Alzheimer's treatments cannot stop Alzheimer's from progressing, they can temporarily slow the worsening of dementia symptoms and improve quality of life for those with Alzheimer's and their caregivers. Today, there is a worldwide effort under way to find better ways to treat the disease, delay its onset, and prevent it from developing. (http://www.alz.org/alzheimersdiseasewhatisalzheimers.asp)

The most prevalent item our family began to focus upon was how we were able to remember parts of bullet I, but moreover how we felt when we realized there was no cure as identified in bullet II. The feeling that hits you is simply stunning. Although the disease has been around, it became much more real to us. You realize very slowly that there is no cure for the disease. The manner in which each family member deals with that is an item to be discussed later.

Once the Google search is completed and the information on the disease is visible form the web search, it is now time to consult with the doctor. Remember the Internet search for information is a process of casting a wide net. We were hungry as a family, so it was automatic to use data accessible on the web. There was a large amount of data

Reader's Notes

• • •

Searching information on Alzheimer's and Dementia will potentially be exhausting. Be patient and cautious of information overload.

_____
_____
_____
_____
_____
_____
_____
_____
_____
_____
_____
_____
_____
_____
_____
_____
_____
_____
_____
_____
_____
_____
_____
_____
_____
_____
_____
_____
_____
_____

accessible and via multiple manners to get the information. There were lengthy theory points, presentations from conferences that users uploaded, and videos on the subject. Another item that made the Internet search useful, was it could access many different items, and the data was increasing based upon additional material being accessible on a world basis. As I reflect, I believe our family used this as our first point addressing the opponent—Alzheimer's disease. Little did we know at that time, that understanding Alzheimer's is not a one-time search and look-up! We had to revisit the definition and align our visuals to what the definition presented—multiple times. A word of caution that we found in our actions, centered upon how the movement of the patient in the various stages. The stages of Alzheimer's are accessible, and you will be able to gain an appreciation of the key items that have been identified. The more difficult item is how that standard is applied to your loved one; as your loved one is unique, and each situation will have similarities, but in that same light will have a lot of differences.

In our case, our mother's doctor was simply awesome. The doctor always made time to answer our questions on site during a planned office visit, via phone call or via e-mails.

Reader's Notes

• • •

I believe you will need to establish a very strong relationship with the doctor, as you will need to balance all of the information from the Internet, friends, and other sources. The medical view from the doctor will assist in normalizing the other input you will get. By the way, you will get an extreme amount of data brought your way. The data you will encounter will appear to be extreme, but a key point is your senses are now more in tune with anything or anyone speaking on Alzheimer's or dementia. Again, using the medical training and experiences of your doctor will be a strong tool for filtering all the information. The doctor will also be able to help you be calm and relax. Our family had to learn this item, which is key. The doctor we used with our mother provided insightful points, as she could see the big picture without emotion. The aspect of having a trusted person who can see the bigger picture and provide words on the potential future actions we would potentially encounter.

The usage of potential is not to minimize but to enforce not all cases will be the same. The research that we did had so many various items, we needed someone to help filter what we obtained from the Internet. We began to understand the additional roles that would be given to each member, not in equal parts, but roles that must

Reader's Notes

• • •

16

be filled. We would urge you to take a few moments now to reflect on your own experiences. Keep your thoughts at this first stage, which is the family's current understanding of Alzheimer's. This is a lesson we as a family learned. Our issue initially was to quickly find the remedy and apply it to help bring our mother back to "normal." Each member of the family would have their approach to the solution, with a central theme of "we have to get Mama back to normal." This high amount of energy with equal amount of emotion created a host of issues. We all were talking instead of listening and respecting the Alzheimer's disease for what it can do.

Understanding Alzheimer's is to recognize the items previously taken for granted as easy actions, discussions, or interactions will change over time. Our doctor firmly provided that guidance. However, our acceptance of the change was so very slow . . . very, very slow. I believe we heard the doctor, but in our hearts we wanted to believe the strength of our mother could overcome the disease. We had no knowledge of the disease, but extreme knowledge of the matriarch of the family—our mother, Luella Pace. I will expand on Luella later, but for this discussion point, keep in mind the doctor has seen a lot, and their words need to be taken in fully, without any dilution.

Reader's Notes

• • •

Increasing awareness of what your family is faced with is helpful. The nature of the disease does have varying effects on individuals.

17

Guardianship of Our Parent

There may be a need to intervene into the daily actions of your parent. Well not daily interactions, let's get straight to the point. Understanding new friends of your parent or loved one will be needed. It is sad to truly understand that there are people who desire to take advantage and abuse the trust that may be bestowed upon them by your parent or loved one.

The amount of publicly available information could become a key wedge for those with untrustworthy intentions to manipulate or gain an unfair advantage of your loved one.

We noticed our mother developing a significant amount of trust in a person who was not in the same age group but of the same gender. Initially, we thought it was good. Our mother had a lady she could spend time with and enjoy herself, as we thought would be good. Little did we know the new friend was attempting very aggressively, in our point of view, to develop a trust that was detrimental to our family.

Looking back at the method of how the friend of mother navigated into her trust, it began at church. Yes, to place of support was a place of infiltration of the new friend. This is not to imply church is bad by no means, but to state how in retrospect being on guard is a continuous task in providing care for your loved one. In our instance, our mother met her friend during a church function service. The relationship grew from guiding my mother while parking to offering rides to various church functions. An interesting time that could be how our mother became so trusting of the new friend. The trusting seemed to grow so quickly, but it could have been more of our mother not working as hard to show she was not forgetting items, as she could easily brush it off with the new friend. The normal items a family member would not think she should have problems with, such as names, special events, or places everyone else in the family could easily recall with clarity.

One of my family members looked at the times our mother was with her friend as an easy way to incorrectly influence and twist her mind due to so much of one-on-one interaction. We are not implying any strange magical process, but moreover just the isolated time together could begin to identify the potential weaknesses. The person or friends of the person could potentially begin to execute their masked motives. Think about how the media strongly urges seniors to be careful of scams. A perspective

Reader's Notes

• • •

Keep in mind you are not invading on privacy, but reciprocating the protection your loved one provided for you when you were young.

_____
_____
_____
_____
_____
_____
_____
_____
_____
_____
_____
_____
_____
_____
_____
_____
_____
_____
_____
_____
_____
_____
_____
_____
_____
_____
_____
_____
_____
_____

19

we observed, focused on how our mother vehemently stated she had been running her life before, and she knows how to judge character of people. This was true in the past, and her strong independence along with a crisp mind was in fact true. But our mother's time perspective was not correct nor was she fully acknowledging that she could be taken advantage of by others. This is not meant to be a sad item, but more of one for continuous use of caution, for the protection of your loved one. Think of the analogy of a passenger in a car, not in control of the direction and will be subject to the destination of the driver. This aligned with our mother, as the Alzheimer's disease was driving, and our mother was a passenger, which reduced her ability to fully control activities. This is to summarize—we believed our mother to be an easy target for those who wished to take advantage of her. This may sound harsh, but reflecting back it is so true. Now the question that I know you are thinking...... "How did you let the new friend get that close?" Well, truthfully, it was our fault, but only because we were struggling also in recognizing how to deal with our mother and the Alzheimer's disease.

Reflecting on the times our family could recall, it would be that isolated time, especially the times when with

Reader's Notes

• • •

Listening to your loved one for the usage of words and phrases, the communication is a key item. Don't worry about grammar, utilize the communication that is being given for good data.

only the two of them were in the car. Additional events/times to our knowledge included walking through the mall together or having lunch together. Our family reflected back and identified a key point was in our belief that our mother could see suspicious actions, as she had always been able to quickly analyze actions of people and determine their intentions. Not always correct, but on point many more times than being wrong. The information just provided was a key item in our weakness . . . not fully grasping how the disease could not only change the perspective of our loved one, but cloud our objectivity in viewing what we see versus what we previously knew about our loved one.

Understanding how each family member may perceive the disease and moreover how each family member's view of the loved one will be different, there is a high potential for the ability for all to fully grasp the current condition of the loved one.

The guardianship of the loved one is a major task that is not an easy one to navigate. Our family noticed items that we believe could be of assistance. The items are not intended to be a comprehensive list but could be useful in your journey of providing care for your love one.

Reader's Notes

. . .

Assessing "New" Friends—Points to Consider (*no sequential order*):

Reader's Notes

• • •

➤ Listening for new names mentioned more than previously known friends of your loved one.

➤ "New" friend(s) does not visit your loved one when the loved one's family is around.

➤ "New" friend(s) does not attend your loved one's family events. There always is a schedule conflict that prohibits their attendance.

➤ "New" friend(s) appears always available to run errands with your loved one.

➤ Especially to the doctor, bank, or other personal business items

➤ "New" friend(s) always provides the words your loved one wants to hear, those words are not reality.

➤ Supporting the idea that your loved one is just as mentally sharp or stable as anyone they know and unsure why the doctor would say otherwise

➤ "New" friend(s) appears very curious of your loved one's financial ability to survive.

Conversation often slides to how much insurance did the loved one's spouse have or how does your loved one live on a fixed income

➤ "New" friend(s) strongly supports your loved one to live on her own in a senior facility

➤ "New" friend(s) offers a perspective on displayed skills of your parent or loved one that is *totally incorrect*—but "sounds good"

➤ This builds a falsehood on the loved one's ability

➤ Examples included driving, handling complex business tasks, living alone, and traveling alone—just a few of the vast possibilities that could be included.

➤ "New" friends reduces time with other friends and attempts to always have isolated time with your loved one.

➤ Inclusion of previous circle of friends reduce.

➤ "New" friend(s) includes your loved one in their family events, without inviting your loved one's family

Strength Becomes a Weakness

Reviewing the skills of your loved one may be an easy task, but take the time to inventory all of those items that made your loved one so special and how strengths were a cornerstone to your family. Gaining a perspective on strengths may be just as easy as looking at your family members, brothers, sisters, aunts, uncles, and cousins. They're more than likely a reflection in some form or manner in your family members. An interesting item our family found was one of the most valuable strengths of our mother began to emerge as a significant weakness.

Our family experienced the independence of our mother was the item that was her best quality. That independence was mixed with determination that made almost any task one that could be solved. Reflecting back, there was the time our mother wanted to make a barbecue pit. She observed how some of our neighbors had theirs built and proceeded to do it herself in the backyard. She used old bricks we had in the backyard, which happened to be the same color. She went to the local hardware store, purchased a bag of cement, and began to build her barbecue pit in the backyard. None of the family could remember her ever having done masonry work or even studied

Reader's Notes

• • •

Identify your loved one's strengths that could become a weakness.

the craft before, but her independence and determination turned a pile of unused bricks into a functional barbecue pit. We can remember how the pit had a unique slant to it. However, by the time our mother finished grilling the food, no one had a mumbling word about the pit structure. Additionally, the sense of accomplishment of our mother was so obvious. If there could have been a comic caption it would have stated "and y'all thought I couldn't do it . . . but I knew I could do it, and I did it!"

The fact that our mother was so independent and determined, contributed significantly in how she would engage with family members during the progressive stages of Alzheimer's. Our mother would get into strong war with words and sometimes even raise her hand in resentment against anyone. It was not all the time, but when she would, it would be difficult to appeal to her sense of reasoning and to also control her physical outbursts. The physical outbursts were more shocking than harmful, but our mother was in good shape, and the impact of a slap, grab, or punch would sting. We were able to find out from one of our aunts that our grandmother acted in the exact same manner, as she too was diagnosed with dementia and Alzheimer's.

Reader's Notes

• • •

Identifying the ability that may have to be taken away will be a difficult one. Understand you could be removing a key item the person had reliance upon.

25

The fact that both had the same disease is important, just as knowing family medical history is always a good knowledge point. What we learned was very influential in our understanding of how Alzheimer's has been observed in our own family. The strength in our family has consistently been the independence and determination. The ability to dig deep and accomplish that item that seemed initially very difficult. The power of independence and determination, enables a person to succeed in many situations, using reasoning as a guide. However, in the absence of reasoning those same traits can become counterproductive. Our aunt reflected back and discussed our grandmother, her and our mother's mother. With a smile, but all along shaking her head and finally just said, "Whew, that sister could be a mean one, if she had her mind fixed on a task, there were not any chance in changing her focus." We used the memories provided by our aunt to help understand more of the journey our mother was on and moreover, not to take what she is doing personal, it is disease using the body we know.

Our mother would often state how if she just had her own house, she would be so much better. She would profoundly state how she had been managing a house for such a long time, there was no reason for her not to have

Reader's Notes

• • •

Keep a calm view of all rational thinking as your view may not be evident with your loved one.

her own place again. But we knew this could not happen, however that would not stop the conversations for occurring. Thinking back, there were some heated conversations about her having her own small home or apartment. The reality was, yes she could do some items on her own, but it was not always in the best manner.

A couple examples of this unyielding independence and determination was her cooking and driving. The cooking, slowly but steadily became not what we knew to be the mouth-watering cooking from the past. This was especially true with the cakes she would bake. The recipes were all from memory. The ability to reason with the ingredients was the measurements she used. Knowing if two dabs of this, a little more than a handful of that, or pouring a splash more of something was needed. When she cooked, it was more of her being conductor of a large symphony and producing a master-piece. The masterpiece not of a unique item, but how she made a traditional item have her signature on it. Those pound cakes are ingrained in my memory and every member of our family. I personally would ask for her to mail me a cake. She would cook the cake and then ever so evenly slice it up for the mailing. The package container of choice was a shoebox lined with aluminum foil. The slices of cake were put

27

into sandwich bags and then carefully put into the aluminum-foil-lined shoebox with newspaper to serve as packing material. The manner she prepared and packaged her pound cakes may have not been taught in any formal shipping classes, but she accomplished the task. I would receive the shoebox package with the sliced pound cake, and I would smile as if it was Christmas. The pound cake was so good, I would put half of the cake in the freezer to save for some time in the future. The cake shipping, receiving, and freezing half of it was symbolic of how the disease actually impacted our mother. You will have to take slices of beautiful times whenever they occur, enjoy them, and save as much as you can in your memory.

The driving aspect was another item that we wrestled with our mother constantly. It was not until our mother had a strange driving event, well it was a single car accident that God did not have anyone else involved. She was driving and just lost focus and drove off the two-lane road and nearly into the steep drainage ravine area. Normally, the area would have more people and cars, but on this occasion it was just our mother driving her little car. After that event, we had to talk to our mother about it. She did not admit to having any issues and stated numerous times that we were just blowing the whole

Reader's Notes

· · ·

event out of proportion. The conversations were not pleasant, but we had to have them as the safety of her and others on the road was important to us. We engaged her personal doctor to assist. This is a good reason to have a strong relationship with the personal doctor of your loved one. We were able to explain what happened to the doctor. Our mother's doctor was very aware of the potential for the removal of driving privileges based upon her knowledge of the disease, other patients, and mostly observing the decline in skills of our mother during her regularly scheduled appointments. The physician provided the document that we thought would help the conversation with our mother. Little did we know, once outside of the physician's office, our mother in no uncertain terms let us know she did not care about a note from her own physician. This is the same physician she once was just crazy about, but now the news not to her liking, she did not want to even acknowledge the physician she selected. She stated she was driving long before the doctor knew her, and she did not even know the doctor, so how could she speak on her driving ability. The latter was another sign that our mother was not fully in control of her mental state. We as a family stood strong and supported each other during the removal of the license and subsequent selling of her car. Be advised the closest member of the family providing care or spending the most time with your loved one, may receive a lot of mean words or have bad interactions. Most of the time it is just due to the fact they are around the loved one more and get the mood changes or wild tirades more than other family members who are not around as much.

The knowledge of a good medical history not the main item, it is the independence and determination characteristics that our aunt explained as being identical. The family historical reference provided by our aunt was very helpful. It allowed the closest family member providing the care to gain a little comfort, knowing the words stated nor the actions observed were directly related to the family caregiver. This was the disease just working its course. When we reflected on our grandmother, it was clear on the changes observed with our mother were reflective of the events our grandmother experience. Although we did not see all of the events, one of our aunts confirmed the items. She provided us good information on how stubborn independence characteristic runs deep in the family bloodline.

Reader's Notes

. . .

Understanding the Time Period

An interesting element of the Alzheimer's disease is how it takes away the ability to align events in time. There are many different ways Alzheimer's can impact your loved one, but how we noticed and dealt with the alignment of events, people, and time was most challenging. The challenging aspect is due to the physical view of our mother would not have you believe she was not in total control, and all was fine. However, what we noticed was clearly a sign, but we did not know it at the time. It began with very slow misalignment of people and recalling the specifics to events. We thought at the beginning it was just a normal part of being a senior, but we learned more as the events became more evident. The identification of events will be frustrating item for family members. As we discussed as a family, each event of how our mother interacted placed a key impressionable item with that family member as the receiver. It made that event so uniquely special. Now imagine that special event you held ever so close and protected in your heart is now not known by the person who made it special. I can almost guarantee that if this is encountered, the effort to make your loved one remember will be draining item for the family member and could make your loved one feel sadder due to the inability to recall.

The internal strength your loved one is using to fight the disease could be impacted greatly by an emotion shot, when their eyes can see the pain or frustration on the family members face. There could even be a few tears in the eyes, due to that special moment that was so important has lost relevancy with a key person of the event. The event may have some of the familiar phases that before the disease we easy memory joggers to find the event being discussed. Phrases our family used included: "You remember what you did . . .", "You remember the time when I was little and you . . .", or "Can you tell me about the time . . ." All of those or even more may be used. But each of those phrases and other ones that could be used do not provide context on the item for your loved one. The reference point previously used to recall the event is missing. The phrases as stated, rely upon a known reference point for the discussion. Each phrase needs that vital input from your loved one, their ability to pull forward or go back in time to get the exact details is a challenge. The disease prohibits the recall of the event. The disease also starts an emotional hit to your family members, especially the person who was the costar of the event with your loved one. What can

Reader's Notes

• • •

The reflection and usage of time is a delicate one. Go to the time your loved one is in versus pulling them to the current time. Write down key points from various decades to help your journey to your loved one.

happen as we noticed with our mother, the presentation of a gentle smile that was wrapped with pain and sorrow. The smile was one that had so many words to explain, but at the end it was all the same. If there was a cartoon caption, I would imagine it would have our mother speaking, "I am sorry, so sorry I can't remember what you are talking about . . ." The other aspect is the family member who was involved in the event. That family member feels a devastating pain point that will linger for a long time. It hurts since that special event is taken as the loved one having purposely forgotten something that was so special. These moments need the entire family to console, and let the family member know it is not them and the loved one did not mean any harm by not remembering. From a practical point, our mother was on to the next item in the day and not having any potential thought any more, after that gentle smile. Our observation was Alzheimer's did not allow our mother to dwell on items. She was back to her own internal fight. Our tasks was to help with the following days and weeks, helping the family member analyze the event without negative thoughts that our mother had purposefully forgot the special event.

As a family, capturing different events in ten-year spans may be useful. Our family used this to help identify what decade our mother was operating in, which then allowed us to curtail our conversations to

Reader's Notes

. . .

meet her in that time period. I started the idea of events in the different decades and used the contribution of the family to help. We found this to be very helpful, if we noticed our mother applying names of different people to current family members. This would often be due to slight resemblience in facial structure, height, voice, or just because it was all she could align in her mind at that time.

In our case, we could also ask one of our aunts to provide information about childhood years of our mother. This was helpful, as we noticed our mother referring to events way back in time, that only one of her siblings could put context around. Conducting the research and documenting the events will assist in reducing what could be called poor memory into more of communciation. We noticed that going to the year our mother was in at that time versus focusing on the current year, helped us have a conversation with her. There is no rule that says the conversation has to be about the current year or items in this current year. We found it fun to just have a conversation, no matter what year it was, so long as we were able to talk about something. Remember the Alzheimer's disease will no doubt prohibit her from recalling the previous conversation, so just go along with it and enjoy the

Reader's Notes

• • •

34

convesation with your loved one. Understanding this type of time travel will potentially be fun, and what we noticed was how just hitting one of the items that could be in the period our mother was operating in brought a warm smile to her face with a twinkle in her eye.

Capturing Key Time Points—Points to Consider (*no sequential order*):

➢ Identify the presidents, governors, or mayors during the targeted decades
➢ Document major purchases—homes, cars, trucks, or home renovations
➢ Document names of neighbors
➢ Document names of special events, parades, or celebrations
➢ Document jobs, volunteer work
➢ Document names of pastor(s) at church, names of members of church
➢ Document family member surgeries, birth (refrain from deaths in the family)
➢ Document the event(s) in the past that normally created laughter when discussed
➢ Document key television programs or movies

Reader's Notes

• • •

Take the time to recall significant events from various decades of your loved one. This will help you have a conversation with your loved one based upon their position in time.

Observing the Decline in Communication

The ability to communicate is often taken for granted, but how quickly it is observed when the challenge is so close to a loved one. It seemed to happen so quickly. One day it was a good conversation, then it seemed to go to a couple of good sentences, then a massive traffic jam of words without context and difficult to understand.

We learned quickly that the conversation may not be the clearest, but it is still conversation. The most important item is to enjoy the conversation and have energy in the conversation.

Thinking back, the decline in communication would appear very strangely as our mother would be talking and just get a little tongue-tied while talking. She would initially just say she had so much on her mind or someone was stressing her out. It was not uncommon because our mother carried so much of the family load, it was easy to believe she was stressed, and we caused the problem. Reflecting more on the years, it is easier to see it was for her the early stages of the disease then began to emerge. The level of how Alzheimer's emerges can vary from one person to another. What our family noticed is how our mother used her strength to fight this item, but it was exhausting to her. Moreover, easier to draw attention as speaking is so easily

Understanding how to communicate will not be static, but dynamic in nature. Remember that the conversation may be fiction-based, but it is conversation. Keep track of good points observed in the conversation, including smiles and overall attentiveness of your loved one.

36

taken for granted. When someone has difficulty in expressing their words, eyebrows begin to raise. The ability to speak words clearly is so basic, that it can be overlooked. Our mother may have heard herself and was so frustrated that she may have used a lot of her energy. Always trying to have the outward presentation of all items being good and that there were no problems. A big item in our family is when you have a problem, you need to sit down, focus, and pray for a solution. However, looking at our mother's fight with Alzheimer's, she may have been troubled more by these events than any other ones. Not diving into medical or psychological analysis, it could have been that she was hearing herself mispronouncing words or not saying what was in her mind that became frustrating. I recall discussions when she would say, "since the doctor put me on that new medicine, I just ain't been right" or "Lord, y'all done worried me so, I can say anything right," and the one heard more than other, "I just need a break, all this pressure on me, I need a break." The message embedded in the verbal statements was "help me." Understanding how our family is not the most vocal in asking for assistance, this was the closest our mother came to actually acknowledging that there was something wrong.

Reader's Notes

• • •

Don't be shocked if conversations appear to be in an unending loop. Keep the flow going with your loved one as the continued discussion is the best element. Each conversation will become a memory . . . enjoy them.

Jumping to later memories, when the disease has escalated much further, the ability to communicate was dramatically changed. The verbal communication became less and less, but the non-verbal communication increased. The type of communication we observed was more of repeating a constant greeting. Each conversation would sound just like the prior one, but it was communication. There is a level of understanding that we had to accept, that is, any communication is good communication. That one was difficult, as each family member wanted a different type of communication or to be able to say how the communication with that person is different. Guidance that we can provide is be ever so cautious and do not get lost in having your loved one communicate on your terms. Remember, your loved one is fighting with all they have, and if the communication may be a little different, well just let it go. Remember, any communication is good communication. Adjusting the threshold and better yet removing the threshold is what we learned to do, and thereafter the communication was a lot better. We stopped trying to measure what was being said, we just enjoyed it. A challenging point can be the infrequent but pleasing times your loved one will conduct themselves with

Reader's Notes

. . .

speech that is reflective of times in the past. Our mother would have days like this when it appeared that time had gone backwards. Our mother would hold a conversation and interact in a manner that was ever so warming to our hearts. However, it would not sustain into a consistent pattern of conversation. Reflecting back on those moments continues to be painful, for it was able to build a fictitious presence of our mother, that was made more larger than it was, by our hearts.

Reader's Notes

. . .

Perspective on Support

Our family became more understanding of the word *support* during the care for our mother. The word *support* not only is directed to the tasks and overall management needed for your loved one with Alzheimer's, but it is on the overall help you will need as you provide care for your loved one.

Loving Support

Being able to provide the constant love during the ups and downs of the disease. This is the warm and caring moments family and friends will pour in. Be advised that this type of support, needless to say must be constant to provide the atmosphere needed for comfort each and every day for your loved one with Alzheimer's. The family becomes the driving focus on this support. The support team members include immediate family, then siblings, cousins, aunts, uncles, neighbors, church members, and friends.

Support/In-Home Care

If nursing facilities are planned to be used, by all means do your homework on the facility and staff. In the review of facilities to be used, it would be good to have a plan A and plan B, in case there is a need for switching services. Additionally, work on all

Becoming familiar with the types of support that will be needed is important.

finances to ensure you have planned sufficiently for the cost of utilizing a facility for the care of your loved one.

We were blessed to find in-home nursing care. The ability to have in-home nursing care was a jewel we did not recognize until we were able to view the services and see how our loved one interacted with the nursing staff. There are many qualified in-home care services, however we found a service we truly enjoyed having. The in-home care service provided by Nursing Companion LLC was jewel we soon realized as a vital element in the care of our loved one. The CEO of the company is Anna Ugochukwu. Anna and her staff delivered services with all of the medical knowledge, but also as if they were family. It cannot be overstated that sound and medically trained resources are needed. Your loved one may not be able to communicate the right items, therefore trained resources will be needed to help identify key elements from focus on events, physical movements, diet, and other activities.

In observing the service delivered, it was done with precision to help our loved one gain comfort in the schedule. The staff providing care was punctual, neat, and respectful, but most of all they demonstrated sincere caring in all the services. If our mother was giving them a difficult day, you would never know

Reader's Notes

• • •

If pursued, finding good in-home care will be a jewel.

41

it. We never observed any member of Anna's staff doing anything that would be considered rude or unprofessional in providing services. Anna led in providing services, included regularly playing spiritual songs for our mother, reading scriptures, and other games/exercises to slow down the disease and make sure each day our mother had fun and enjoyment. Anna was even able to get our mother to sing spiritual songs and understand our family traditionally only worked on the usher boards, we are not singers. However, Anna worked with our mother to get her to blast out tunes and smile in the process.

The in-home care also assists in having medically trained personnel around our mother to help provide information during her primary care physician visits. We were also able to utilize Nursing Companion LLC for memorable quick rides out of the house, which provided our mother one with an opportunity to enjoy the fresh country air. The ability to have a consistent set of faces around our loved one was the jewel we recognized later was a truly good blessing. The in-home care molded their services into the home in a manner that made the in-home care services feel as if they were family.

The services provided initially were just during the day, but as our mother's health deteriorated it became

Reader's Notes

• • •

The range of support could vary, be mindful and utilize those that will best fit your loved one.

helpful for overnight services. We expressed our desires to Anna, and she worked to have her staff meet our needs. We utilized the services of Nursing Companion LLC up to the last day of our mother's time here with us. If you are planning to utilize medical staff for in-home care, finding a jewel as we did will be essential for your peace of mind and moreover for the special care of your loved one.

Administrative Support

This support centers on the day to day operation points needed to help manage the unseen but key points of the overall environment needed with you loved one with Alzheimer's. In our case, the administrative support was with the Primary Care Giver. This was due to our mother residing within the family versus being at a care facility. During the time at a family's residence, it is key that the administrative work is done to keep the medicine on a steady basis, observe the dates for doctor appointments, make sure the clothes are maintained, laundry completed, special meals, manage sitting times outside or in a park, and all of the items that are done on a daily basis. These are small items, but when the contribution effort is viewed throughout the year, the total work becomes much larger.

Reader's Notes

• • •

Business Support

This support focuses on the level-headed and non-emotional activity that is needed. The Alzheimer's disease is growing with understanding, and with that more types of medicine and care is becoming available. However, with the emergence of good, there will be cautious areas where the business support task will be needed. The business support will also need to be ready to serve as a power of attorney. It is needed for this role to have their own business items in alignment, so focus can be provided to the complex items of the loved one.

Spiritual Support

This support is very delicate in delivery, as it depends on the spiritual-base of the loved one with Alzheimer's and that of the family members providing support. This support area will provide the communication to the church or religious establishment the loved one was a member or visited. This role will also need to have the awareness to provide the needed remote spiritual support in case the loved one is not able to attend church services, coordination of attending via online services, or contacting members of the church for their potential visit to your loved one. We found the visits by members of the church or various clergy very good

Reader's Notes

. . .

for our mother and made us feel very good.

Listing of the Supports:
- Loving Support; Nursing Support; Administrative Support, Business Support, and Spiritual Support

Reader's Notes

• • •

Relationship with Primary Physician

The relationship with the primary physician proved to be a major point of strength for our family. The strength we believed was due to the ability of our physician to have a keen eye on our mother's condition over time, but also to have such a heartfelt care for the family. We were extremely fortunate to have Dr. Veronica Patterson as our mother's physician.

The physician will provide the medical information and continuous assessment of your loved one's health. We valued the neutral and very astute perspective relative to what she has observed with other patients and her exposure cases of Alzheimer's. It is good to keep the awareness that the information received has to be aligned in the correct manner, and don't lose sight that your loved one may not fit exactly into a stage or category. Keep the points mentioned in the chapter "Understanding Alzheimer's," which will help you and your family from being potentially overwhelmed with data. Your loved one's physician will not know how you are processing the data and moreover how your emotions are influencing the processing of the data. We learned that having access to information is useful, but keeping a clear perspective of what we observed

Reader's Notes

• • •

Establishing a good relationship with your loved-one's physician.

In you notes make sure you have all the contact information – phone, cell, email, etc.

with our own eyes was good. This also helped the physician, as it provided more data points for comparing to other patients with Alzheimer's.

The relationship developed over time with our mother by the grace of God finding the Dr. Patterson. Dr. Patterson and her supporting staff were all very good and friendly. An interesting item is the office staff carried the same warm and personable manners as Dr. Patterson. You may not always get the complete package, that being the doctor and staff being warm and friendly, but if you do, it will be a great benefit to your loved one with Alzheimer's and your family. Our family had numerous calls with Dr. Patterson, asking questions, getting opinions, and just overall support. A side benefit from Dr. Patterson's office was the amount of attention she provided on our family from a caregiver perspective. She would point out at various times how the disease not only impacts the patient but the care-givers. I can recall how after an exam for our mother, Dr. Patterson provided concerning points on the potential impact to our family, especially the person our mother may see the most. She was direct in stating how the closest person will get the wrath of our mother, numerous verbal attacks, and it could become physical in nature. The family member

Reader's Notes

• • •

Leverage the medical knowledge provided by the physician, to obtain insight on furniture or other special needs the physician may have background and/or ability to connect you with a good source for purchasing. Also, inquire if the physician to visit the home if possible.

who would be the farthest geographical distance away, may be appear to be the saint. Nevertheless, she warned us on how the disease would continue to progress and the likelihood we would experience the same items. Again, having a physician that is truly concerned on the patient and the patient's family is a blessing we received. We also received the same from Dr. Patterson's office staff, as demonstrated when there would be prescriptions needed or medical billing questions, they always had the time to talk with us, using as much time needed to address all of our questions and just to have a friendly chat.

We were fortunate that Dr. Patterson's patient care was so down to earth in delivery, it is a strong factor in having confidence in the medical services being provided. The medical services provided to our mother was also good for each family member. We were getting educated on how services can and should be provided. Each of us, with that thought I really want a physician like Dr. Patterson to be there if I require the same medical attention. We silently prayed we would not require it, but being able to observe the medical treatment along with the progression of the disease with our mother was extremely good for the family.

The relationship with the physician may also be of assistance for when

Reader's Notes

• • •

48

obtaining needed supplies or furniture, if care for your loved one will be at home. Utilize the physician's knowledge on good medical items that will be beneficial during home care. Dr. Patterson even made visits to the house, to get a visual on the environment and delivery of the old time physician care to our mother. The visit made to the home was an item not asked for from Dr. Patterson, but we truly appreciated. It had the feeling of a friend just stopping by to make sure all is good versus a physician.

Reader's Notes

. . .

Family

The items in this section may be difficult to consider, as it is family looking at family. No matter how much objectivity is used, it is still difficult balancing emotions and objectivity will require significant energy and internal fortitude.

Our family notice items about our mother at different times, due to the busy calendars everyone maintained. Our reflective points in this will not be the same for everyone, due to each loved one who may have Alzheimer's was a unique person before and will be yet another unique person with Alzheimer's.

A point we acknowledged in understanding, was the first time it really hit home that our mother was sliding away. Based upon everyone in the family, having different interactions will at some point be a startling item, when it is so crystal clear the loved one you knew is not there. Our mother physically looked great, but that was only on the outside and the person on the inside had gone. I can recall each of us having that moment, and it seemed to be a point of major news and a requirement for us to communicate that item to other family members. I believe the best advice is to allow each person in their own

Each family member will have a unique perspective due to their unique relationship with the loved one.

way acknowledge what Alzheimer's has done and don't try to shut the family member down or minimize what they wish to express. It may not be clearly obvious, but the communication by that family member will be somewhat of good therapy for them. Understand in their mind they have accomplished a major goal. They are facing directly the impact of Alzheimer's. If you try to minimize their conversation or not listen to them, it can be a devastating item that may not be very visible. A point to watch is all of the family will have ups and downs on the emotional roller coaster, so when there is a time to provide support, please do so. They may be the family member who is always the strong one, but don't take them for granted. When a member of the family wants to talk about what they have observed, listen, listen, and listen.

Reader's Notes

• • •

Family—Constructively Let Off Some Steam

The journey in providing care for your parent or loved one will be a taxing item on the family. Keep a good listening ear for hosting family meetings to keep all on the same page. Notice the reference to staying on the same page, as the reference. It may be difficult to "all" have the same exact view, approach, thought path, but you must keep the family directionally together.

We noticed in our family, we became a bit on edge. The basis may have not been with our mother's fight with Alzheimer's, but to potentially items from the past. Our approach to this was a family meeting. The framework of the meeting provides all very few details when initially announced, but just emphasized everyone's presence at the meeting is a must.

The meeting was held right after we celebrated our mother's birthday, where we showered her with flowers and love. The meeting structure was gathering around the table, everyone pulling up a chair. Each person was handed a New Year's noisemaker that you blow air into, and the air unwinds a tube and produces a sound. A toy horse was in the center of the table, along with a bottle of whiskey and a bottle of wine. No note-taking or other printed material. Everyone was also

Reader's Notes

• • •

Ability to enable family members to discuss what is on their minds in a manner that keeps them revealing and others listening is key.

52

asked to stay engaged and listen with their heart.

Each family member was given a small glass for a drink before we started the meeting. This was just to help get everyone loose, since the purpose of the meeting was not provided in advance. We allowed each person to just speak freely on issues, appreciation, unsure of actions anything and everything, but there was a caveat. The person speaking maintained the floor, if someone had comments, they would blow into the New Year's noisemaker. This was done to allow the family member speaking to maintain the speaking time and not have someone overrun their time. This was so helpful as it provided the family member the entire time to unload and not worry about another person taking their time or talking over them, which would lead to them shutting down. The toy horse would be used and laid on its side, if it was being viewed as an issue has been "beating down" and let's move on. We had a lot of tears shed during the meeting and lots of sounds from the various New Year's noisemakers, but the horse was not placed on its side not one time. Upon the conclusion of the meeting, we all prayed together and hugged each other. Each family member extended similar thoughts as it was a good process to let off some steam and that they were not

Reader's Notes

. . .

interrupted, which helped their thoughts to continue.

Recognizing everyone does not have the same speaking styles or abilities is sometimes lost. Therefore, creating an environment for the family member to have the floor without being overtaken is a good recipe for the person to open up. Additionally, the other family members will have no choice but to listen. The energy for blowing air into the New Year's noisemaker may exhaust them.

There may be a need for multiple meetings or other types of events to help, depending on the family, this can vary. A major item is that there has to be a person within the family that can provide the objective view of the whole environment and know when the discussion time may be needed or other events to help keep the family directionally aligned, which will ultimately help in the care being provided to the parent or loved one with Alzheimer's.

Reader's Notes

. . .

The Damage to the Family Member Providing Primary Care

The role of the Primary Care Giver (PCG) is critical in the caring of your loved one. Before jumping directly into the PCG, let's walk through the roles of members. This is not a medical type analysis of roles, but mostly what our family found though the years and with information referenced online from time to time.

The identification of the PCG was not difficult to determine, but what we did not know would be the amount of mental and emotional stress that would be placed on the PCG. The PCG has the fortunate and unfortunate positon as being so close to the loved one with Alzheimer's. The immediate item is that it is better that nurses, as our mother would have a familiar face. This is good. Well, actually the perspective of familiarity is from an external view and with a rational mental state. The perspective of our mother was opposite to this, thus not what we had planned. Our mother would have days of strong verbally abusive language. The true basis of the abusive language was the idea of putting rational thought onto our mother. Over and over, this approach would serve as the basis for more mental stress.

Once we consistently aligned the words being spoken as just words not having direct malice, we were much better. The range of words from our mother went from early teenage years—the 1950s, the 1960s, the 1970s—and sometimes reflective of discussions with her siblings. The rationale may be understood, but when you are the recipient of the verbal outburst, it can have a stinging impact. The item that makes the impact so stinging is when the PCG is a family member, that family member is not expecting the attack. The outbursts can totally surprise the PCG and hit an exposed nerve. The PCG is mentally thinking of providing the best and maybe looking for one more good conversation, and lo and behold, they get verbally attacked. The PCG can be so taken back that it distorts the care that was being provided. The attack also may be a consistent one, that the PCG must understand and constantly know the attack is not directed at them, but at the person the PCG appears to be from the loved one with Alzheimer's.

The PCG is a very important position, but be very observant to help the PCG when it appears the verbal attacks are having more of a negative impact on the PCG. When we observed this in our family, we arranged for the PCG to have a quick weekend vacation.

Reader's Notes
. . .

Anything other than being close to be subject to a potential attack. The time away is also good for the PCG just to recharge their battery, as the role that they have taken is a totally consuming role.

An item that we observed is the prolong time the PCG was viewing the negative impact of the Alzheimer's disease can have on the PCG. The negative impact in our case, was our PCG projecting themselves in the future with Alzheimer's and how we would treat her. This was not clear until a consistent theme of the conversation was "I hope y'all . . . for me." Once we could listen to our PCG closely, it was clear to see it was a distress call. We had fun about the way we would treat our PCG, and she laughed and understood. We had learned too much with our mother, not to be in a better position to provide even better care to the next family member when required.

The PCG will no doubt slide back into the projection into the future and visually see themselves in the positon of needing care. When you see this or hear it from the PCG, address it quickly. The PCG distress call is one to address and resolve quickly. The sustained health of the PCG is critical, so do not take it for granted and keep a very close ear for the distress calls. The PCG is carrying a lot that is visible with the care, but even more are the feelings and/or fears that may build up on the inside. Allowing the PCG to have time of solitude when they don't have the daily responsibilities placed on them is important. A quick trip away or just time in a nice hotel where they can let their guard down to relax will be an extreme help.

The opposite of the PCG is the "golden one." Whoever this is has to recognize not to get lost in that role of being the one that can do no wrong. It may be due to geographical distance away, characteristics, or just by chance the loved with Alzheimer's has placed a halo on the person. Whoever gets the title must know it is only a fictitious label that has been applied. The loved one with Alzheimer's was just classifying people in the best manner they could. Remember the PCG needs all of the support, and that person is "golden."

Reader's Notes

. . .

The Decision of Hospice Care—Yes or No

Examining a definition of hospice: 1) a lodging for travelers, young persons, or the underprivileged especially when maintained by a religious order; 2) a facility or program designed to provide a caring environment for meeting the physical and emotional needs of the terminally ill.

The second meaning is the focus of this section. This is only made easier if you have become more accepting of the devastating effect Alzheimer's can have on the quality of life and that full recovery is not an expectation built on solid and rationale thought.

Our family arrived at the decision in a short amount of time. We thought what would we want if we were in our mother's position. The ability to have surroundings that are more family would provide an environment for the rare occasions that an appearance of our mother from years gone by may emerge. We collectively agreed that being in the home versus in a remote location was the avenue to pursue. This also meant that we would increase the hours of the homecare nursing team to reduce any unplanned work on our PCG. The home care nursing team was added to seven days a week during the day and three overnight coverage during the week. The additional

59

homecare will increase your homecare expenses, but you are approaching the sunset of your loved one. The decision must be holistic and be a firm one. Our decision was holistic, as it included our feelings, what we thought our mother would do, and the quality of nursing homecare just to name a few. We were all committed to pitch in more to make the times as best as we could. The home environment also made it easier for the long sitting sessions, just looking at our mother and holding her hand from time to time. The home environment also enabled any visitors to quickly go in to visit, without having a room limitation, etc. We truly believed the home environment made a difference. At different times, our mother would give us a subtle nod of the head or an eyebrow raise, so it was almost as if she was saying "I appreciate what y'all are doing . . . thank you." In all actuality, we knew she was gone, but the interpretation we obtained from some of her gestures was all we needed to know we were doing what she would have wanted.

Reader's Notes

. . .

The Key Business Items to Address

In this section, there are two very direct messages. The first message, take the time to determine who will be the selected person to serve as the power of attorney (POA). This activity should be addressed during the time your family member with Alzheimer's can fully understand and confirm those wishes are in alignment with the POA. The creation of a POA can be a complex or easy one depending on the requirements of your respective state. It would be good to Google information and/or call an attorney for guidance on the best route to pursue.

Upon completing the POA, make sure you have digital copies and additional certified copies available at the home where your loved one with Alzheimer's resides.

The second message of this section is more on the quality of life item. The documented instructions should your loved one's vital signs require medical assistance (loss of heartbeat or stop breathing). The term most widely associated with Do Not Resuscitate (DNR) documentation. The DNR is a legal order providing the directions of the afflicted party, should there be a loss of breath or loss of heartbeat, and the usage of cardiopulmonary resuscitation. The medical support personnel will request for the DNR guidance, should there be an event. The ability to document the wishes of your loved one is essential. We took the time to use the discussions our mother would have about the cemetery plot she purchased years earlier. The discussion was not a pleasant one, but we knew it had to be discussed for a clear direction. This is an item your loved one's physician can also assist. Dr. Patterson was very helpful in explaining DNR and providing sufficient items to complement our own research. The physician will not decide for you, but will provide key points based upon their experience that can be leveraged during the decision process.

Upon completion of the DNR document, make sure you have digital copies and additional certified copies. Storage of the POA and DNR in a plastic sleeve, mounted on the wall is a reasonable location. This would make the document readily accessible, should the need arise.

Reader's Notes

• • •

The Final Arrangements

This section may be the most difficult section initially, but as you prepare and accept the journey of your loved one, the activity may be easier.

During past discussions with your loved one, you may have been able to know the answers to the questions below.

- Vault burial or cremation
- If vault burial, all of the preparation associated
- If cremation, all of the preparation associated

Before any other items are done, there should be consensus on the type arrangement, otherwise confusion could consume the already tense situation. Once a decision is made, you will need to identify a responsible and trusted company for the funeral services. We chose a local one in the area and had numerous meetings a year in advance of our mother's departure. We believed the early planning and ability to outline our expectations assisted the funeral services team a great deal. All of the planning has to have a good funeral services team engaged to be accountable to the agreed-upon plan. Our point of advice here would be take your time and find the right funeral

63

home so you can meet your objectives completely.

If the path of cremation is chosen (as in our case), we would strongly urge a member of the family get the task of locating a good picture. Upon agreeing on the picture, engage a printing shop to create a large picture that can be placed on an easel. We utilized a picture that was more symbolic of our mother as others knew her, as this is the last memory we wanted to give all who are attending the home-going services. A benefit with the cremation, is how the family can control the visual items and how the life can be more celebrated using the selected picture posted on the easel. Each of our family members stated the picture of our mother and home-going services was an experience they would treasure.

We utilized a funeral home that had a strong family approach and helped tremendously on the planning. The Gregory B. Levett & Sons funeral home was superb in delivery knowledge, trust, and peace of mind during the entire final arrangements process.

Reader's Notes
• • •

Summary of Memoir Discussion Topics

Reviewing the journey taken, using our family memoirs:

1. Understanding Alzheimer's
2. Guardianship of the Parent
3. Strength of Character Becomes a Weakness
4. "Understanding the Time Period"
5. Observing the Decline in Communication
6. Perspective on Support
7. Relationship with Primary Physician
8. Family
9. Family—Constructively Let Off Steam
10. The Damage to the Family Member Providing Primary Care
11. The Decision of Hospice Care—Yes or No
12. The Key Business Items to Address
13. The Final Arrangements

Although the reading is done, keep in mind each and every moment, discussion, picture with your loved one, will be items to cherish.

Reader's Notes

• • •

Now the reading is done, remember life is an action. Keep that in mind and enjoy the times with your loved one.

Share your notes with your family members. You can also add their points to the various chapters as the collective views will be useful.

_____
_____
_____
_____
_____
_____
_____
_____
_____
_____
_____
_____
_____
_____
_____
_____
_____
_____
_____
_____

Closing Thoughts

Our family hopes that our sharing will provide some assistance and/or affirmation on your journey. The varying aspects of the Alzheimer's disease are bad, but we trust and believe in the power of the family. Even the smallest task is strong and supports the strength of the family in providing care to your loved one. Keep in mind your loved one may not speak direct words of gratitude, but remember when a smile does appear or a gesture made, you will know it means thank you—keep and cherish it!

If the loved one could have said goodbye, without a doubt they would have done so. Therefore, with all your heart and with a smile, understand that your loved one by no means intended to hurt anyone, it was only that the loved one . . . just forgot to say goodbye.

About the Author

Robert L. Pace is a senior information security and compliance executive, with experience spanning over multiple decades in the industry. Born and raised in Detroit, Michigan. Robert received his bachelor of science degree from Michigan State University, master of science degree from Walsh College of Accountancy and Business Administration and executive leadership training at Thunderbird School of Global Management.

The educational training was helpful, but moreover the love and strength of their family served as the core element needed for the caring for their beloved mother in her fight against Alzheimer's. Robert's pen to paper is a reflective view of how their family learned, struggled, and bonded together in tackling the ups and downs of the devastating disease. The journey of the family provides basis for his new book.

CPSIA information can be obtained
at www.ICGtesting.com
Printed in the USA
BVHW050041291121
622756BV00019B/667

9 781642 583960